For Women Who Roar ™

Megan Febuary

FWWR Publishing

yourbookyear.com
forwomenwhoroar.com
meganfebuary.com

Library of congress control number: 2020922763

ATTENTION BOOKSTORES AND SHOPS:
Interested in distribution of this book? Discounts available for bulk orders.
Please email info@yourbookyear.com for more information.

To all of you brave and afraid, you are
stronger than you know.

I've been writing poetry since I was eight years old. Hours spent hunched over dictionaries searching for language that voiced what I couldn't say. Each word, a way to get the poison out. Each phrase, a little more truth. Each poem, a validation of my unsayable experience.

This poetry book is what inspired For Women Who Roar, the magazine and the movement. This collection weaves themes of grief, healing, and trauma recovery. May this collection be a reminder that your voice matters, your story matters, you belong here.

xo, Megan Febuary

contents

Illustrations by
Caitlin Metz

Scars

there is a young wound in me crying out
"how can i heal you?" i ask
with a small stutter and an open hand
the wound replies "embody me"

-embodiment

memories fly away faster
than they land
so i grab them by
their fluttering tails
till the wings fall off
i wish i'd let them go
now these memories lie
still in my hands
and i wonder if
i should bury them

-the burial

carry my pain
you ask without asking
eyes sagging and wet with longing
and i did

i drank your pain like liquid poison
bloated in my belly
bloodshot and blurry
drunk with feeling
not my own

after a short time
i walked away for what felt like miles
while i watched you fade in the distance
light as a feather
floating easy
a breeze of a body

there my feet filled with lead
back hunched
holding the weight of what was left of you
regret, shame, sadness
so much impossible to name now

when you're ready to return
find me here
deep in the dirt of another life
dig me up

and all the parts of you
ready to be recieved back

i will rise from the lightness
of no longer needing to be the closet
you stuff your soul in
to hide your darkness

on that day
when i return
carry my pain
i will ask without asking

-carry my pain

when i was little
my brother brought home
snapping turtles
as big as a house
i was terrified
until i became one
hard on the outside
soft on the inside
hidden by a shell of armor

-snapping turtle

go ahead
pour foundation on
like thick honey
you can't cover the scars
that start from the inside
thank god because
they're fucking beautiful

-show me your scars

maybe if i had been cold
instead of warm
maybe if i had frowned
instead of smiled
maybe if i had hunched over
instead of standing tall
maybe you wouldn't have
taken my kindness
as a permission slip

-permission slip

woman
you are wild
and fierce
and restless
like waves that have lost sight of boundary
breaking over rocks with a crash of disrupting beauty
people stop to see you moving

woman
you are soft
and gentle
and flowing
like a smeared sunset in a fire lit sky
people stop to see you healing

you are both
brave and broken
hard like ice
yet melting like snow

this is your time
this is your dance
i'll meet you shaking on the floor
where we can be free

–brave and broken

soul wrapped in skin
you have survived
this body war
and have birthed
beauty from scars
most of which will never be seen
etched internally
a map of a life
no one can fully know
except you
body
holder of space
healer of heartache
handmaiden of truth

-handmaiden

i am a deep
deep cave
inside golden
and they rob me clean

-i never asked to be treasure

i saw a bottled vanilla coke today
and it made me think of you
brother
dark hair
long face

i hate vanilla coke
but at lunch i bought it
because i missed you so much

one sip and i thought
i could drink you there
but i couldn't
and the aftertaste
only made me more lonely
more aware

-vanilla coke

they were there
they weren't there
they were there
they weren't there

god, they were there
that's the most painful part

-the disappointment

when did my vagina get so old
and grow elephant ears
that could fly off my body

-something changed

i can feel the tears hovering
like thick rain clouds gripping
white knuckles
holding an ocean of resistance

who told me it wasn't safe to cry
that i should smother any sign of saltiness
that the keeping in would be better than the letting out?

-the resistance

how do you reconcile your loneliness you ask?
i dip my fingers in bourbon and stir

 -it doesn't really work

sometimes
when i get really lonely
i put my mouth against the mattress
and whisper all my regrets for the day
i imagine my pillow is a lap
and fall into a sleep
brought on by the comfort
of thinking someone is there

-the aching

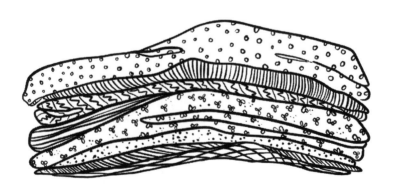

on the bus a man walks by
his body dipped in a pack of pall mall
making him smell just like my uncle
he had a house made from a deck of cards
with toothpicks holding it up

i used to visit every summer
smoking cigarettes and searching
for the twenty-five kittens
hidden under the front porch

i was eleven
getting high
popping pills
getting high
popping pills

i barely remember any of it now
just that i left with chemical burns
the size of texas on my brain
from huffing so hard

yeah i was running
running from the inside of my body
trying to find a way out of stories i couldn't tell

-house of cards

open hands
i could fit in there
you know?

curled up
and put in your pocket
like a piece
of blue lint
that rubs raw till it's fragmented

i could be
whatever stays close to you

-blue

once upon a time
there was a girl
who opened herself
to men like a pin-up
to watch them awe

i am her
roaring my trauma
watching men open me
from across the room

i run away
and chase them
with no clue
where we're going

 -dissociation

i remember when it wasn't like this
helicopter rides on thick carpet
my ankle hitting the corner hall
it hurt a little

you would smile often then
happy teeth and bright pink gums
it made me imagine exactly what you looked like
when you were little
now so much older
you seem sad

i'm sorry for the pain
i may have caused you
that's never been talked about
only felt
on long walks
with grass climbing up to our knees
and hot air
like a hug holding you

-helicopter ride

i watch from the bathroom door
leaning my little body against the frame
peaking over the vanity chalked with dust
my mother pours tan liquid from a tiny glass bottle
rubbing foundation on her fingers like wet paint

she is an artist

i watch her cake layers across scarred skin
how the oil fills each dimple like a pothole

layer one
half a bottle on face with a thick line
where pale white meets burnt orange

layer two
pink blush on a brush runs across thin cheeks
particles fill the air and fall like glitter
i try to catch them

layer three
blue shadow across heavy eyelids
and cheap mascara on little lashes

layer five
encased powder pressed on skin
Poof poof poof
the sound of a face disappearing

layer six
bright lipstick
rubbed lightly against thin lips
only the bottom and a smack
magically the top lip is painted too
slightly faded and off center

everyday
my mother colors herself
everyday
she hides

everyday i watch
witness and wonder
if i too will become an artist
trapped in a mirror

-the artist

i've forgotten
what it feels like
to be touched
i don't even recognize
that it is hunger

-longing

anxiety
is tipping
like a cool
glass of water

c
  r
    a
      s
        h
          i
            n
              g

wet shards
on the wooden floor
i'm sorry
i couldn't catch it

-the apology

don't dissect my story
like a science project
just because you
don't like what you hear

you have your truth
and I have mine
one just happens to be
more true than the other

-scalpel

suddenly
i
was
a stain
that couldn't
be removed
on your favorite
t-shirt

-resentment

once you spelled out
i love you
with chopped up almonds
on the kitchen counter
you didn't say it though
you never said it
but scooped up the letters
into your hands
and ate them whole
i figure that comes close to telling me
if you believe in eating your words

-almonds

brother, do you love me?
big tan calloused hands
that push me into a carpet burn

brother, do you love me?
joints rolled thick and tight
like your middle finger

brother, do you love me?
eyes painted red and blood smeared
into your hairline

brother, do you love me?
a hard punch through my bedroom wall
and fuck you's like a chorus line

brother, do you love me?
drug urine tests for holidays
a gold star for a good sister

brother, do you love me?
late nights spent by your bedroom door
waiting for the gun to click

brother, do you love me?
slow sexy bodies
swaying on a tv screen

brother, do you love me?
salt water up our mouths and noses
I rode on your back like a dolphin ride

brother, do you love me?
thick threaded silence
and secrets that scream

brother, do you love me?

you love me
you love me not
you love me
not

-gold star

memories fall off
like temporary dragon tattoos
i try hard
to stick them back on
but they won't

s   t   a   y

-it's blurry

my eyes
are beginning
to look like my fathers

a pool full of grief
i was never allowed to swim in

SPLASH

-swimming pool

i knew you were home
when the bottles started breaking
outside my bedroom window
like an alarm clock
going off every night

i got up to see you
with your bloodshot eyes
and smoky mouth
mumbling words
indecipherable

the way your tongue
swallowed and spit
each letter so deliberately
no one could tell what you were saying
though I tried hard
to decode meaning from madness

i was desperate to know you
desperate to save you
brother
from the white powder
the bourbon breath
the barrel gun
tucked into the top of your closet

so that's what i did
i saved you
for one whole year of your life

my twelve year old body
took off your shoes
held your hair
and tucked you in like a baby

do you remember?
it was the closest we've ever been

-the alarm

hands large and wrinkled
hold me in place as I cry
then suddenly

g   o   n   e

-absence

what's the secret hidden within you?
the wound
the gaping wound
the wound with voice
and color
and feeling

the wound
rising up to be healed
when you name it

yes, this wound
this secret
this sacred opportunity
to step outside
of the silence

-it hurts to heal, but it's worth it

Cages

i know it scares you
to see me get angry
to hear a woman
scream and howl
and lose her mind
but i've been told
to be quiet most of my life
voice muffled and whispering
so now i'm yelling
every chance i get
to make up for the silence
like a lion
let loose from her cage
roaring and free

-for women who roar

my daydreams are laced
with how i might burn myself
and watch the smoke rise
because you o' lord
delight in burnt offerings

-bad religion

i made the mistake of telling a man
i wanted to make art with menstrual blood
and he looked at me like i was crazy
he doesn't know how it feels to pour
that hot wetness between my thighs
how it shows up monthly
like a desperate mother
still i'm surprised every single time
that she comes knocking
scraping at my door frame
like some wild animal
he can't know how it feels to bleed
from the inside of a sacred womb
shedding layers like snakeskin
to make room for new life
or
        maybe
                    not
he doesn't know
the stain after stain after stain
on panties
on bedsheets
on body
after unwanted sex
this stain that's been waking me up at night
for the past 25 years
he can't hear society's shaming
to put it away

that scarlet garment
dipped in bleach and dissolving
so long there's holes in it
speaking of
i need to go shopping for underwear
as black as the last day i bleed
so i can camouflage the shame
this is how my body roars
with thick oil red
that turns to watercolor pink
flowing out of me like a fountain
no i don't need a paper plug to silence me
i need a bucket
a paintbrush
and a canvas as tall as you to create on

-the bleeding

who cuddles a porcupine?
the masochist

-i thought it was love

i want to be free
but freedom is linked to desire
desire has been tied to shame
shame married to violence
still they felt safer than comfort

-the conflict

i haven't written anything since you left
in truth i haven't known what to say
i didn't expect to see you
with long hugs
and the desperation burning in your eyes
so puffy and so much older now
i didn't expect you to talk so much
to be so full of
       e v e r y t h i n g

i pictured you how i saw you last
with your emaciated spirit
so thin
like your soul had been sucked
right out from your body
a walking ghost
bloated with regret

but now you're full
with alcohol
so strong
it pushes right through
your blood stream like a river
and you ride that current in
like it's a fucking waterpark
to be honest
i've never seen you look so free

every once in a while
i would look back
and see you trailing behind
with your face red like a lobster
hot from sun and cholesterol

taking long sips
from a plastic flask
shoved deep in your pocket
you drink it like air
and i get it
you must need to
to live with yourself
with the rage
with the shame
in order to
survive

-the plastic flask

i hope you can see me
through the layers of chaos
shades of red
tinted blue

i hope i can touch you there
through walls of words
climbing high
falling apart

no more towers
or tanks
or tools
to make ourselves other

just you
me
free
and forgiving

-layers

don't try and domesticate me
i am a wild woman
made to be free

-lion lady

i was born backwards
eyes wide and bloodshot
taking breaths with bubbled cheeks
like a blowfish
face pressed against a glass tank
i was the surprise child
the first girl
the youngest of three
the baby
pale skinned female
with blood and puss
face loose and wiggly
i had no vocabulary
no context for shame
just baby faced and free
no one warned me about the flushing exit
from a warm womb
like a plug pulled fast
making me tilt-a-whirl down
a dizzy vagina drain
no one told me about forceps
that would dent and bruise my skull
till I was a month old
or about the cold metal salad tongs
cutting my cheek
no one covered
my innocent retinas
from the florescent lights that
burned like foreign fire

or the freezing air
that made my pure skin
grow goose bumps for the first time
they just pulled me out quick
looked at my vagina
gave me a name
and cooed
wiping the red from my body
like they were embarrassed
covering me
in white cotton
and handed me to aliens
big white aliens
aliens with eyes like mine
that sagged and drooled slobbery tears
aliens that held me and rocked me
back and forth
back and forth
a soothing sway I still do today
back and forth
back and forth

-i was born backwards

sky stretched slow
like an old man rising
and i'm just waking from sleep
three years deep in a foggy cloud
you keep guessing the shape of
it's me in four different outfits
that i thought you'd recognize by now
me in your favorite shorts
torn and baggy
wrinkled sweater
put on backwards
your sister's socks
hair knotted
stripped and smiling
in about five minutes
i'm going to stretch and splinter
into a thousand tiny pieces
this is me
breaking apart
in front of you
this is my irreverent explosion
and my passive voice
asking you to come in

-the explosion

stress has been occupying
my body for the cheapest rent
i should charge more

-bad roomate

i write for the woman
who suffers in silence
who fears her voice is gone
after decades of misogyny
her mouth taped
hands tied
weighted down with bibles
too heavy to lift
but still asked to carry

i write for the woman
who still feels the ache
who tastes the salty grit
of a memory
turned sour and spotty
his sleepy eyes
thick fingers
mining a dark cave
searching for gold
but she never gave permission

i write for the woman
who swallows the small blue pill
who smiles outwardly
yet inside wars a battle
that no one can see
her buttoned up shirt
Small scars
carved deeply
in the bathroom stall
but now hidden and healing

i write for you
because i am you
silenced
aching
swallowing
but still
we are rising

- i write for you

poetry is not meant to be polite
if mine is polite
then blow it up
i want to make beautiful messes

-the poet

my earliest memories came late
with no flash flood warning
the deep water swept in
while i was sleeping
filling my nose
making me choke

i thought
i might just die here
i might just drown
from a memory
that i didn't want to know

-flash flood

tears
a salty ocean tide
rising in my cheeks
they roll in
crumbling mental sandcastles
and roping fantasies
with sticky seaweed
i am the wet sand and hollowed door
dug out by a toddler's hand
the imagination born
in fragile rooms that hide
and duck in corners
i am the quick collapse
under the weighty blue curl
hovering soft
hovering hard
you are the water
dark deep water
rallying rhythms
that gallop and stomp
the walking threat
in crocs and a smile
eye of the storm
center and strong
you are the coming and going
coming and going
the tidal wave
and the hallelujah clap

together
we are crashing
always crashing
the masked collisions
and the slamming of breaks
together we are blending
always blending
the mother moth
caught in the corner web
tears caught
not taught
mitigated
not mused
words folded
scolded
branded
accused
i am the tears
i am the words
i am
you are
blurring
the ocean in eyes
brought on by the current

-sandcastles

i crawl into myself
chin tucked
i hide
i'm everywhere you are
daughter
bone of my bone
flesh of my flesh
woman
child
woman hidden by child
big country accent
buttery smile
i slip
i fall

my mind is a war panel
when I think of you
Shots blast
explosions in my memory
center of my world
hand on shoulder
kiss on head
i become other
hot bath
i become steam

do this
in remembrance of me
but my memory is cauterized
and what I do remember
terrifies me
flip flopped
fucked over
truth turned
and tossed
like a cheap salad
leaving you hungry
for more
more
more

-remembrance

we lived for that bottle every night
red wine filled our bellies
like a round swimming pool
lips and teeth purple too
sometimes they would break
and we would step on sharp things
tiny sparkly fragments
like glitter that stung
i still feel them sometimes
that little poke of broken glass
reminding me why

-addiction

it's hard being a woman
silenced and small
it's hard to tell the truth
when you won't listen

-cover your ears if you need to

create the boundaries
that get you liberated
lose the boundaries
that keep you locked up
freedom is choice

-open the prison door

tonight
i know
every crack
and tear
and hole
i know
the distance
between
each picture frame
the dense smell
the tilt of my lampshade
i know
the whistling rattle
my fan makes
when it gets too high
the sound of looseleaf paper
like it's set on fire
this room
a familar womb
where i'm warm
fetaled
wet
reborn
each morning
every night

-hypervigilance

three things i believe
we are full of light and shadow
we are sometimes free
and sometimes caged
we are all made for love and belonging

-a new theology

you are allowed to change
to unravel
to become
undone

you are allowed to shed
to grieve
to shake
wildly

you are forever becoming
who you are and who you were
always meant to be

untamed
uncaged
feeling and free

-reminder

awaken
a fire within me
turn this freezer
into flame
light the coals
beneath my blue body
till i become ember
bright red and burning
it's time to exchange
this numbness for desire

-i'm ready to feel something

don't let desire
dry up in you
caked and cracking
stand in awe of the desert
but be washed
by the river

-baptism

sadness hangs around in the evening
i'm too polite to tell it to leave
too awkward to ask it to stay
it piddles around my basement
puts his feet up on my favorite orange chair
and makes me a Totino's pizza for only $1.55

-the other bad roomate

short breaths
small lungs
can't sleep
can't eat
can't let you love me
a well of loneliness
in a room full of people

so many words to say
no mouth to speak them
breaking apart
but still holding
all the pieces

-night sweats

what's wrong with your skin?
the kids yell down the hall
did someone hurt you?
the teachers ask me in quiet corners
so i begin wearing long shirts and baggy pants
that cover my discolored skin
how the patches that form look like a quilt of color
on my inner arms and thighs
in the doctor's office
the man with thick glasses
smells like penicillin
i wear a red and white two piece swimsuit
under my clothes because my parents gave them
permission to use my body as an experiment
so he turns up the florescent light and pulls a black
polaroid camera out of the second drawer
snap
the front
snap
the back
snap
the side
lift here
bend here
breathe here
then he blows these photos up as big as times square
for men with more thick glasses to sit and stare
at my body at a long table lined with tall chairs

when i was little i prayed i would be famous
that people would look at me and stare
with an ache of curiosity
i just didn't think this is how it would be
and so i changed the prayer
that no one would know this strange girl
with the strange body
looked at by strange men
that loved studying strange skin

-polaroid

Voice

i wrote my first book
when i was twelve
and it told the truth
so they threw it away
along with the stories
they told me not to believe
but i kept writing
telling the truth
going to battle
to uncover my healing

writing became my warpaint
with it i fought the message inside
that said you won't make it
even now i'm fighting those mantras
with boxing gloves so heavy
i dare you to lift them

-boxing gloves

infants cry
and make horrible expressions
no one tells them
how silly they look

as children get older
they run to pillows
to hide their blotchy faces

someone told them

-shame

a mannequin
that is me
dipped in beige and porcelain
posed and pretty
fingers slightly bent
knees deep in scalding water
Jaw dropped and silently muttering
break me open
i need more air

-break me open

if

i

forgive

will

it

make

the

truth

less

true ?

-the risk

i plug my ears and go deep inside
the only sound is the dull hum of silence
like a womb and the water surrounding it
here my breath sounds like a respirator
and it makes me think of you
on that hospital bed years ago
with a tube in your chest and scars
so fresh i could still smell your bleeding
it was hard to see a strong father
turn skinny so fast
to watch your eyes grow wide
scared and full of feeling
you'd never shown before
suddenly a body full of truth
but no mouth to speak them
that room was a smothered gray
so depressing the color
as sliding doors
opened and closed
with a monotonous beeping
made us all anxious
mama sat close to you for hours
worried lines drawn into her eyebrows
like with a pencil
did you know
she watched you
even while you were sleeping?

we thought you might die there
brother and i
as we leaned hard
against the wall
feeling faint
like a feather
the way it slowly falls
and crashes to the floor
we thought we might not say
the sorry's we never had
or hug in a way
that was more than sideways
always pulling out
rather then caving in
but you didn't die
didn't even come close to dying
you rose out of that bed weeks later
with a scar on your throat like a pirate
full of body and bones
and the same silence
lying dormant
in the well of you

-but you didn't die

sometimes you write a story
sometimes the story
writes you

-the process

for all of you
who know the struggle
of dark days
even when the sun is glaring
for all of you
who try to speak your truth
and no words
can escape your open mouth
for all of you
who feel that relentless hunger
no matter how full
you've become
to all of you
who believe in god
but feel too angry to pray
for all of you
i hope you know
you're not alone
not today

-this is for you

i've begun stammering
the more honest i get
i can tell i'm getting closer to truth
when when my words play
like a
like a
like a
skipping record
truth has a way of doing that
hijacking articulation
and trapping the tongue
how do you put language
to such violence anyways?
it's like paintings of windows
replacing actual windows
you see oil colored trees and blue swirling wind
but you can't feel it messing up your hair
these are stories that are visceral and real
language that breathes and bleeds
that is both terrified and aroused
i am a stuttering storyteller
glorying in her own obscenity
cutting down the curtains
letting the light in

-skipping record

if my vagina could talk
what would it say?
get the hell away from me
you touch nice
but play mean

i'm a baby

i'm a baby

i'm a baby

-baby talk

we can't be the couple
that no longer talks in public
who sits across the table
eyes averted
with voices that have gone into retirement
we must stay wild
and make love in ridiculous places
are you with me?
it's time to destroy all that distracts us
meet me on the edge
of that bridge we used to go
and let's throw our phones
into the river

-meet me on the bridge

dear darkest day
you no longer define me
i am one with the light

-genesis

i wore heels a lot then
and cut my bangs shorter
than i meant to
we told stories
for the first time
over bourbon drinks
and apple pie
from a nearby super market
late nights and legs draping
everything new
voice
sound
smell
expression
you'd play music
in the background
that we'd fall asleep to
i heard one of the songs last night
and remembered that feeling

let's go back there

-return

i let poetry pour out of me
like a drain
few words
much meaning
makes me feel more
then I'm used to

yesterday I wrote about
how visceral fading feels
and cried publicly
tears running down
the back of my throat
no one noticed

again
the drain

-pouring

and then it came
the laughter
so startling
what I thought had been buried
now baptized
resurrected
and bubbling up
from the well within me

-renewal

remember the time
we yelled for days
until our throats were sore?
then the pitch quiet
not even the sound of breathing
regret so heavy
it smothered words
too impossible to say

that's when you grabbed my hand
and pulled me close against your heart
THUMP
THUMP
THUMP
the only sound
i needed to hear

-heartbeat

there are some words
when said out loud
that make you stutter
some strands of sentences
so brave that your mouth
must pause to awe

i started stuttering a few years ago
when i began to tell the truth
who knew stuttering was so sacred?

this is what happens
when you tell stories
from the ground up
you breathe in
the grit and cough
it reminds you
that you're human

-sacred stutter

some days
are so dark
they make you tremble
lord let there be light

-a prayer

i was made of dirt and sand
pieces of glass and shiny stone
soft sharp and intentionally crafted
by rough hands and painful fire
no I did not give you
permission to shape me
yet you shaped me
over many years in suffering silence

will you now pour water on this dry skin
and watch me become sacred clay?
slightly cracked and glossy
this is our holy opportunity
to heal what's been heartache

-the potter

i'm not a captive
i'm the captain

-taking back the ship

my body is a pen
spilling ink
my life is paper to be
written upon
my will moves the pen across
the page
look
i can read my life

-storyteller

inside my mind
an intersection

inside my body
a manuscript

inside my spirit
a river

-trinity

at some point
you let your voice retire
before it was ready
now so much silence
every once in a while
you hum out of habit and smile
then catching yourself
you hit the breaks and cry
that quaky lip once alive
now dry and frowning

-early retirement

my hands are too big
and wrinkled
for this story
my body
a million ages
screaming its truth

-the truth within you

shake
tremble
loosen
the old chain
your daddy wore
when you were young
that he asked nicely
if you would carry for a time
with your body bent over
from years of yes
now you stand tall
with the clicking tongue
that won't stop saying no
to the old chain
that no longer fits
because you have outgrown him

-the old chain

some stories make us shake
like an earthquake
so seismic
this truth
when we open our mouths
to share
this repressed rupture
rising up
from the deepest of places

-earthquake

when i was little
my friends called me sunflower
with long straggly hair
bleached in all the wrong places
i wore baggy blue jeans
and my brother's t-shirt
that hung down to my knees
smearing my mother's eye shadow
across my lids like a magazine
i was an old soul twelve
but looked around eight
crooked teeth and gappy smile
hanging around all the wrong kinds of people
i was desperate for someone
to see through the thin skin i was wearing
to call out the imposter in me
so i could be free
my life felt like an ongoing game
of hide and seek
except i was the one hiding
and no one was seeking
how terribly lonely
can you imagine?
this is around the time
i began to write poetry
and it felt like being found

words upon words upon words
piled high like a blanket
i crawled under
and lived there
with a village of stories
perhaps I never left
because here I am
still writing
decades older
with a little less hiding
still going by the name
sunflower
every now and again

-nickname

no one will write that book for you
no one will create that art
sing that song
or take that trip
you've been talking about for ten years
this is your life and what you make of it
today you decide
will I be awake
or will I be sleeping?

-awake o' sleeper

words are small
today i only have two
thank you

-gratitude

my eyes have seen
a body dressed in thick robes
face red with blotchy tears
hand on small shoulders
as a mother disappeared

my eyes have seen
blood on the sidewalk
after a hot day at the pool
with people gathered around
to stare at the boy who slept on cement

my eyes have seen
the underbelly of a mattress
covered in soft stains
creaking from the moan
of a young promiscuity

my eyes have seen
red eyes filled with smoke
in a tan oldsmobile
that my oldest brother drove
down a tired road i forget the name of

my eyes have seen
jesus's mouth covered in blood
laughing over the steel table
of open heart surgery
as he kissed these open wounds

my eyes have seen
the little girl
crouched at the end of a long hall
rocking back and forth
back and forth

my eyes have seen
my eyes have witnessed
my eyes have known
all that's forever unspoken

-my eyes have seen

Courage

i might be small
but my voice is not
my desire is not
my truth is not
my soul most definitely is not

today i shrink for no man's comfort
it's time to grow
from this glory i am made from

-let's rise together

here we go
into the wilderness
the chaos
the restless ache
the hunger
i'm not afraid of it anymore
are you?

-it's not as scary once you name it

i hope you find him
and that he hugs you
like when he was young
without regret
or even a hint of shame
i hope he doesn't pull away too fast
at the fear of being loved
after years of living
in a lonely cave
surrounded by an ocean of beer
i hope you don't feel
that sting of loss
that pricks like needles into skin
that you've felt for years
since he left without a word
i hope you don't have to search too hard
only to find nothing
but a lingering smell of him
i hope you have conversations
that go deep as dirt
and that you will speak
about broken things
i hope you leave with hope
not more weighted sadness
and that you will see a son
once dead
now resurrected
and returning home

-the lost son

little blue salvation
dissolving on the back of my tongue
washed down by faucet water
rinsing my desert throat
i belong to a generation of blue women
who swallowed the pill whole
in hopes it would save them
from sadness thick as sinking sand
in a once pitch black room
now lit with wide open windows
a light where there was only darkness
a blue river
for the blue women
who bath in it without apology

-blue women

someone told me
i am resurrection's daughter
i smiled
burial grit
browning my teeth

-daughterhood

people keep telling me i'm brave
but i can't stop shaking

i'm
       so
             afraid

-a new kind of courage

i don't move away like I used to
when you hug me
the way i'd squirm
when we stayed to long
restless legs
anxious heart
how they used to shake so furiously
now your strong arms and warm body hold me
loving like it's the last time
who knew you would be such a sanctuary?
with that button up shirt
and hair that fell so wildly
my love
a cathedral of stained glass
slightly broken on the edges
sharp and brave
when you touch me
i feel everything
the good
the bad
the beautiful
all of it
i feel the feeling
i used to run away from
but now i stay
because it's safe to

-you are a sanctuary

you are full of light and shadow
you are not swallowed up
you are rising

-both / and

i step in
that's how it begins
one pinky toe dipped in wet paint
then a foot
a hand
a body submerged
i fall in
that's how it ends
all my insides on the outside
dressing a blank canvas
it's a mess
i don't try to clean it up
i'm a mess
i try hard to clean me up
the artistry lands between the two
like an exaggerated crack in the sidewalk
where we play four-square
with slapping hands and mimicking smiles
they are all stories
like decoupaged life layers
that we crawl under and cuddle beneath
on blistery days
this art is where I roar my life
i've been caged after all
now I break the bars and pound the ground
here in expression
we can make drumming sounds
with beats that make a million colors

like a burning bush
the secrets of our life
fan the creative flame
i'm taking my sandals off
and throwing them in the fire
it will make the smoke rise
we need more light
we need more signals
we need more shoes to throw in the fire

- the invitation

i rise and fall
like soft waves crashing hard
against splintered pylons
the sound of hope
roaring
you can't quiet the ocean
the wildness of its tide
oh how i've tried
to smother its voice with my body
hurdling into the sea
but hope is bigger than this body
bolder than my fear
braver than my determination
to bury it alive

-the sound of hope

stop trying to hold the world
and instead
hold yourself

-self-care

that summer was cold when i visited you
leaves fell like fall even though it was late july
you picked me up from an old train station
just like in the movies and we hugged awkwardly
like it was the first time
it had been eight years since i saw you last
both of us changed so much
we barely recognized each other
your face puffy
wide and grinning
slightly balding and a walk like a waddle
my face thin
freckled and frowning
dreaded hair and body unbathed for days
you said i looked like a hobo
and i took it as a compliment
that night you made your special spaghetti with cinnamon
and we talked about family things
traveling and god
so normal it was nice
later with bellies full of beer
you asked me to sing you a song
i only knew one
an old hymn about a prodigal son
who had run far away from home
listening and humming along
you cried
tears i'd never seen before
now falling so freely

-the prodigal

i see you
unraveling
th knots of who you were
to embrace the freedom
of who you're becoming

it's beautiful

-in dedication

there's something magic about you
the grime
the grit
the glow of the sidewalk
the sirens
the subways
the sound my boots make on the concrete
there's something broken about you
something chaotic
something always being rebuilt
that says you belong here
if you want to

-the city

so you're afraid to do what you love?
me too
let's do it afraid
let's be the brave ones
that keep showing up
after everyone else stopped
when they felt something difficult

-fear is the teacher

at night
my body begged
to be submerged in water
when the night terrors
made goosebumps
stand tall on skin
and i would run miles
in circles from something i cant say
round and round
these little legs would take me
when i awoke
body full of sweat and salt
covered in blankets
piled over my head
i stumbled out of bed
still dreaming in circles
desperate to wake
from the sleepless sleep
i made my way down the long hall to the bathtub
and turned the hot water on to boiling
put one toe in
then the other
and let my eight year old self
become both water and steam

slowly i awoke from nightmare
to find myself in a womb
of my own creation
safe
sound
secure
in the deep submersion

-bath junkie

bravery looks like
loving the girl in the mirror

-reflection

i will
when you can
open yourself
and i can move through you
be the vessel
and i'll be the holy water
pouring

-open

let me be brave enough
to step into the deep water
icy cold and waves crashing
i have no capacity for shallow words
this neutered truth
give me ocean
wild and roaring
take me to the depth
i try hard to avoid
and let me swim there
with the secret things
salty seaweed and creature
yes this holy pain and healing
this sacred invitation to dive

-deep water

everyday i wake up and ask
will i be swallowed by a narrative
that broke my heart?
or will i stand as one whose stronger
more fierce
and growing
because of it?
your stories have power
but so do you
today you choose the story
you are becoming

-you decide

i thought i had moved on
but your memory hangs tightly
like a shadow
in the door
along the staircase
tucked away
in each dark hallway
every time i come close to forgetting
that shadow shows up to remind me
this is how i know i'm close to the truth
i feel the feeling i'm no longer numb to
i shiver at your ghost
but i don't run away
i taste death
but i breathe resurrection

-the haunting

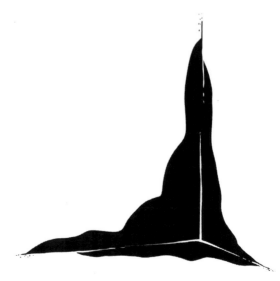

break open the dry ground
pull out the weeds that block you
bloom tall and bloom fiercely

-keep growing

about the book—

For Women Who Roar is a collection of poetry
and prose about healing trauma and uncovering
one's voice after the experience of silence. This
book is split up into four parts: scars, cages,
voice, and courage. Each section takes the
reader through the heartache of trauma, pain,
and ultimately recovery. Written by writer,
writing coach, and Founder of Book Year and
the magazine For Women Who Roar, for whom
this poetry book prompted. I hope this collection
speaks straight to your soul, the light, dark, and
all the in between places.

 Xo, Megan Febuary

about the author—

Megan Febuary is the Founder of For Women Who Roar and Book Year. As a writing coach and healing healer, she has dedicated her life to helping women write their books and heal their stories. She has published 1000+ works of women, edited and curated 10+ literary magazines, and coached hundreds of women in writing, healing trauma, and creative direction. She is currently working on her next book.

Printed in Great Britain
by Amazon